THE ADVENTURES OF
PEPITA MORALES
AT CITY HALL

THE FIGHT TO SAVE EL JARDIN.

Written By K. Mayenbeer Cruz
Illustrated By Carmen Osorio

This is a work of fiction. Names, characters, places, and incidents either are the product of the author's imagination or are used fictitiously. Any resemblance to actual persons, living or dead, events, or locales is entirely coincidental.

Copyright © 2021 by K. Mayenbeer Cruz

All rights reserved. No part of this book may be reproduced or used in any manner without written permission of the copyright owner except for the use of quotations in a book review. For more information, visit www.kmayenbeercruz.com.

First paperback edition 2021

Illustrations copyright © 2021 by Carmen Osorio

ISBN 978-1-7378233-0-8 (paperback)
ISBN 978-1-7378233-1-5 (ebook)

Published by K. Mayenbeer Cruz

www.kmayenbeercruz.com

For my tribe.

It was Monday. The beginning of the week at City Hall.
The day started early for Council Woman Pepita whose job is to continue to build a better community for all.
Pepita was working on finalizing the last details of the community's annual Dia de Carnaval when the alarm went off.
"Council Woman Pepita!" screeched Lucas, the chief of staff from the lobby.
"¡Rapido! We are being overrun!"

Familiar faces began to gather outside the Council Woman's office.

"¡Aquí estamos! ¡Y no nos vamos!" Pepita rushed to address the crowd.

"¡Mi gente!" said Pepita. "What is going on?"

"Pepita, they are taking away our jardin," replied Nikko.

"¿Chiquito, qué dices? What is going on with el Jardin?" asked Pepita.

"The City wants to sell el Jardin to Mr. Big Box so he can build a shopping center," said Sara the Baker.

"They left a notice outside el Jardin's gate," added Miguel the Painter. A gloom fell over Pepita as troubled faces looked up at her... waiting for her to speak.

"Mi gente, don't move! I will be right back," Pepita cried out to the crowd as she returned to her office.

"What am I going to do?!" bawled Pepita. "Our community will be devastated if we lose el Jardin." Pepita became disheartened. "The people are counting on me to help them. I don't know what to do," she confided to her four-legged friends.

"Pepita, remember what Abuelita told us when we felt sad or scared," said Charlie the Cat.

"You fight!" replied Lola the Cat.

"No."

"You run!" said Gizmito the Dog.

"No."

"You hide!" yelled Gizmito the Dog and Lola the Cat.

"No!" replied Charlie the Cat in dissatisfaction.

"We breathe, listen to our hearts, and look for strength in our ancestors."

Pepita remembered. She remembered the many lessons her Abuela had taught her about their past, the lands their ancestors came from and traditions that were passed down from generation to generation.

"Recuerda mi niña, we are not alone. Whenever you feel sad or scared, close your eyes, take a deep breath and feel the loving energy of our ancestors," said Abuela.

Pepita closed her eyes and placed her right hand on her heart. She took a deep breath and stood still.

"Abuelita..."

"Mi niña, no tengas miedo. We are always with you... guiding and protecting you.
Listen to your heart.
That is where you will find your power," said Abuela.

Pepita opened her eyes wide and yelled with glee,
"Let's go save nuestro jardin!"
"¡Lucas! ¡Rápido, ven por favor! I know what to do!
We are going to get all the community together and together we are going to organize a march and community meeting to save nuestro jardin!"

Pepita and her four-legged friends ran with excitement to let the people gathered outside her office know the action plan.

"¡Mi gente!" Pepita addressed the community.
"Don't fear! Together, we will save our beloved garden!
We will use the power of our collective voices and we will lead with our hearts!
Are you ready?" Pepita asked the crowd.

"Yes!"

"¡Si!" cheered the community.

"Nikko," said Pepita. "Tell all your friends what is going on. Tell them we need them."

Miguel the Painter, make sure todo el Barrio comes out to support.

Sara the Baker, we are going to need a lot of arepitas to fill our tummies.

"Together, we will show the power of the people and together we will win!"

"Yes!" cheered the crowd.

March to Save el Jardin

The community gathered to march in support of saving el Jardin. The children made colorful "¡Si Se Puede!" posters and hung them along the march's path.

Lupe the Science Teacher brought maracas and tambores.

Pepita placed her right hand over her heart. She looked up to the sky, closed her eyes and took a long, deep breath.

"I'm ready," she whispered.

"¡Mi gente!" Pepita addressed the community.

"Are we ready?"

"Yes!"

"Let's do this!"

Community Meeting

"¡Bienvenidos!" said Pepita.

"We will be hearing from the community if the City should sell el Jardin to Mr. Big Box or keep investing in the garden as a public space.

The City will decide after everyone has had a chance to speak."

The room fell silent. No one moved or said anything until the first person was called to speak.

Sara the Baker went first. "We must keep investing in our garden because el Jardin feeds us. We grow berries, tomatoes and delicious herbs like cilantro and basil," said Sara the Baker.
One after another, the members of the community raised their voices in support of keeping the garden as a public space.

Miguel the Painter said, "The artists in our community use el Jardin as a source of inspiration. We must protect our public spaces."

"My mother takes my brother and I to el Jardin to play after school," said Nikko.

"We love to swing from the peach trees and play in the water sprinkler."

It was now Mr. Big Box's turn to speak.

"Hello, everyone. Don't worry. Once I take over the garde——Oops! Did I say that?"

Mr. Big Box placed his hand over his mouth and let out a soft chuckle. "What I meant to say was, when Big Box is built, the community will not miss the old scruffy garden."

"I would like to say a few words," said Pepita as she stood up from her seat.

"An entire community has come together to support el Jardín, a magical place that benefits us all. From the little ones who run around and play among the peach trees, to the elders who spend their days cultivating the land so we can have crops year after year. We must save our garden."

It was time for the City to cast their votes in favor of keeping el Jardin or selling it to Mr. Big Box.

Pepita received the final vote and moved closer to the crowd.

"The people have spoken, and the City heard us loud and clear. Our community has rejected Big Box!" The crowd erupted in cheers of "¡Si se Puede!"

"Mi gente, today we showed our power. When I say people, you say power!"
"People!"
"Power!"

"People!"

"Power!" joined the community.

Día de Carnaval

The next day, the community celebrated with bright costumes adorned with feathers, bows, and gems. Dancing masks glided up and down the parade, while music played out of vibrant, colorful floats.

Pepita looked up to the sky and smiled brightly. Pepita's ancestor smiled back. "You did it, mi niña. You used your power, got the community together and helped save el Jardin."

The end.

Meet Dolores Huerta

Fearless labor and civil rights leader. Creator of the slogan "¡Si Se Puede!"

Dolores Huerta is a labor and civil rights activist who has spent most of her life fighting for better working and living conditions for farm workers, immigrants and the most vulnerable in our communities. Dolores is a firm believer and advocate for political organizing to effect change.

In 1972, she co-founded the Farm Workers' Movement which sought to secure better working conditions for farm workers in the state of Arizona.

After Dolores was told by many that the rights she wanted to achieve for farm workers could not be done, with bravery she responded, **"¡Si se puede!"** and the famous slogan was born. **"¡Si se puede!"** has become the rallying cry for those seeking to enact change and make our communities better.

Dolores was born in New Mexico in 1930 and continues to fight for equality in the Latinx community.